Relationship

This Was Not My Idea

Emily Howe, RN

ISBN: 9798342206860

Acknowledgment

Thank you, Jason,

Thank you, Gwen,

Thank you, Mom and Dad,

Thank you, Leah,

Thank you, Kara,

Thank you, Anik,

Thank you, Andrew,

Thank you, Kim,

Thank you, Debbie,

Thank you, Jamie,

Thank you, Anne,

Thank you, Kathryn,

Thank you, Vanessa,

Thank you, George,

Thank you, Cristy,

Thank you, Lynett,

Thank you, Sheilagh

Thank you, UCP of Maine.

Dear Diary,

Today, my boss pulled me aside and drew a picture on the whiteboard in the small conference room at work. The one down in South Wing at the ELC building in Bangor, Maine. He began scribbling furiously on the board, all the while telling me how he couldn't sleep, and he just had to tell me this idea. His hands flew around the whiteboard, explaining the cover of this very book that you are holding in your hand right now.

He also constructed the framework or skeleton for the chapters in this book. To say he has been supportive is a gross understatement. He is a coach, mentor and really, really good guy. This book is dedicated to him. He also shares the first name of my dearly departed younger brother. I think that they wouldn't mind sharing this dedication; they would have liked each other.

All my love,

Emily

To Andrew,

Thank you from the very bottom of my heart.

Emily.

To Andrew,

I miss you from the very bottom of my heart.

Emily.

Page Blank Intentionally

Table of Contents

About the Author

Emily Howe, RN, Assistant Director of Nursing with United Cerebral Palsy, has connected people of all backgrounds for over twenty years through advocacy, recovery, community service, and leadership training. A veteran of the US Air Force and a graduate of Eastern Maine Community College with more than 13 years in the healthcare industry, she brings valuable insights and techniques for building strong, resilient relationships to the organizations and individuals she works with.

A seasoned healthcare professional with a harrowing personal journey including poverty, recovery from drug and alcohol addiction, and life as a young, single mother, Emily credits her education, relationships, and community as the driving force for developing her own resilience and recovery. Passionate about helping others and investing in her community, Emily brings people together to learn, grow, and develop into the best partners, employers, colleagues, and humans they can be. Understanding, empathy, and education cultivate long-lasting success. Emily brings these elements together in her consulting and coaching work as you embark on your path to a sustainable future with a workforce that has employee satisfaction.

Page Blank Intentionally

Foreword

Some of the words in this book may be from my own original ideas, but I don't think so.

There will be an exhaustive list of thank yous in the book; feel free to kick me in the shins if I forgot to mention your idea that you taught me along the way. It mattered.

Elemental Consulting

www.elementalwithemily.com

Chapter 1: This is Not My Idea

All the things that I have to share with you come from my teachers. My teachers are everywhere around me. Mostly, my teachers are my family, friends, coworkers, patients, and even my pets. I have learned things in classrooms as well, and a few important teachers come to mind who will cringe at my writing style, but they'll forgive me because they love me so much. I'm thinking specifically of the amazing Kathryn King, Assistant District Attorney, former history and policy teacher, mock trial and track coach, and dear Mr. David King, of course, who taught history at the same high school in rural Maine when I was attending in the early 1990s. They cared very much about our futures, and it was easy to tell.

Mrs. King and the best of the teachers along the way have taught me to challenge authority, question facts and resources, and always strive to be curious. I am happy to sit and talk with anyone about just about anything, but I get all fired up when people *want* to discuss how to build healthy relationships in any capacity. Relationships are *everything.* The rest of this book will be supporting evidence in both anecdotal and published research. The people who did the research will be thanked appropriately. I have no interest in reinventing the wheel, and I am very grateful for their diligent study and commitment to share the information with all of us.

I'm sharing with you the book list I have been marinating in for the last year and a half or so, and I hope to express my sincere thanks to these authors and give them proper credit for giving me so much support in my journey:

The Happiness Advantage by Shawn Achor. This book is so important to me. I'm so thankful he did all this research for us all these years. This book is also an easy read, so go ahead and pick it up or get the audiobook. It's narrated by the author, and that is always a special treat. My biggest takeaway from Shawn are the 7 principles of positive psychology, and we'll talk about that more in this book, probably ad nauseam. Shawn teaches us how he learned that happiness is the state we are in when we are striving to reach our potential.

Connection by Nicholas Christakis. This guy is Shawn Achor's mentor, so I had to know what he had to say. Excellent work and research; I highly recommend it. This one reads as more of a case study and less of a series of stories, but it has more of a clinical feel. Taking an anthropological lens when we look at our social and cultural behavior and communication techniques helps to build more contextual understanding and shrink the divide between different groups. The Us vs. Them thing is less relevant and less intense through that lens. This book made me think in a very zoomed-out way.

Dare to Series by Brene Brown and her work on shame and empathy in a book called I Thought It Was Just Me (but it isn't). If any of you know Brene Brown, would you pass along my thanks? She is providing us with language to help process complicated feelings that are so critical for building healthy relationships. This is how we change the world in these moments of connection. Brene Brown is honest, raw, and open; she sets a great example for me of peaceful truth-telling.

Turn the Ship Around by David Marquet is full of lessons/stories about leadership and how incredible the workforce culture can be when you are focused on building leadership qualities in every single person. He teaches us how he learned that leadership shouldn't be exclusionary and that the job of management is to provide the opportunity for everyone to be successful if they choose to do their part.

Oh, and the book that Dave Grohl wrote, Storyteller, when Taylor Hawkins died, I felt so sad about that and found his stories about growing up and growing into himself to be a captivating read. I have zero personal connection to the musician or the band except for the relationship I have had with their music, which is and has been incredibly rewarding, healing, nurturing, and educational. RIP Taylor Hawkins. (Dave, if you read this, come back to Maine and bring your drums.)

My regular work is in management. At present, I work with Certified Nursing Assistants, and I love it. I also support a Home Health and Hospice nursing team, and this work is wonderful because it's so easy to see that in this business, there's more to the world than just randomness when you are working with the ill and dying. I do some community work through my faith community and the peer support recovery community on a regular basis. In all the work I do,

I essentially do the same thing, and that is to build connections between people. I have a knack for making new friends, and I'm great on the microphone. I'm good at finding words to facilitate developing your own ideas/thoughts about yourself. I started providing training and education in this community in the early 2000s when I began teaching a class for an internet connectivity support call center in Orono, Maine. That place taught me a lot, but that's a story for another book.

Over the years, I have worked with some wonderful teams, helping to develop a curriculum targeted at supporting women who are new in recovery to gain and build on skills to self-advocate at their doctor's office or in the courtroom. They need skills to be able to tell their story with purpose in a way that the message is clear and the intention is felt with relevance, such as how to talk about their history when in a job interview and how to recognize their value and their innate resilience and leadership skills in hopes of increasing opportunity and access for these women new in recovery. This could heal the community if the cycle of substance abuse and poverty could be broken through peer support and reaching for their potential.

In 2024, I officially launched Elemental Consulting, LLC. The reason Elemental with Emily exists at all is because of my darling husband. He is so sweet and patient with me as I analyze every single conflict we have, every single time, ever, and forever, for the last 15 years. The name of this book might end up being *My Husband's Brain Injury Taught Me How to Talk with People.*

Looking back on October 23rd, 2004, my soulmate (whom I hadn't met yet) was in a head-on collision with another, larger motor vehicle. His injuries were extensive, and they could not find any signs of life at the scene of the accident. One EMT decided to go to the scene of the crash, even though he was just leaving his car to head into a movie and reached to turn the radio off as the call came in… or the story goes pretty close to that; I wasn't actually there. This angel of a man found signs of life in the broken body, and my would-be husband survived and continues to live without his left leg, which is amputated above the knee, a frontal lobe traumatic brain injury, and the physical and emotional scarring from many injuries and trauma. He has the coolest scars, and he's funny and handsome; just ask around. My husband is a talented and widely respected dog trainer; animals love him. Some people are born to play violin or paint, but my husband was born to help us love animals. You know he is a good person, especially way down deep inside because animals just love him.

Well, my darling Jason struggles with communication and all the things associated with the frontal lobe – which is essentially everything to do with interpersonal relationships. When we first decided we were going to be married, we negotiated how we would fight with each other. This was not my idea. Jason said to me something like,

"When you leave me, make sure you tell me why because every time a relationship ends, I feel shocked, and I never get to understand why."

Well, I don't mind telling you that I was stunned at his ability to just blurt out how he was feeling. I have struggled with that my whole life. We launched into a discussion about how we like to be approached when there is tension or unresolved hanging ugly feelings. I need space and time with my feelings. Jason wants to have all the feelings out loud all together and plow through them so it can be over. I will say cruel things if I'm not careful with my words. I'm better at it these days because, well, I'm older for one thing. For another thing, I'm not living in fear, and I don't hate myself or secretly fear that people don't *actually* like me. Don't get me wrong, I tell myself terrible things all the time; I'm just not living with those particular voices in my head at this time. So, we discussed this when we were not emotional at all. We said to each other that we should just remember that, duh, we'd never want to hurt each other. If we could get back to that thought, we could check ourselves and maybe even re-approach with more peace in our hearts and in our words. As for Jason and me, we simply agreed to choose to believe each other when something is wrong. For example, he might say to me,

"Babe, you're acting crazy."

And I chooooooose not to speak; I choose to take a step back and consider that perhaps I may, indeed, be acting like a crazy person. He loves me; we are on the same team, and we want the same things. We agreed to try to understand each other when he needs closure and to charge through the mess while I need space and time so that I don't say horrible, mean things (which is my coping from old trauma crap and not the truth). We often struggle and stumble through painful conflict, but we are so much better at it than we were before and better all the time. We have grown to like each other more over the years, too, and as you can imagine, that really helps things. Did I mention how handsome he is?

This is the origin of my desire to learn more about humans and why we do/say/think/feel the things that we do. Throughout my grown-up working life, I have been a supervisor, a manager, a trainer, and so on. I have been working and learning how to reach people to help them learn; this bloomed in helping each other learn about ourselves. That grew into developing great teams, people working together in that magical space where the pendulum swings near the center and work gets done. This would wax and wane, and I would wonder why people didn't just act like me. Things would be so much simpler! I remember telling my therapist something like that, and he said to me, "Emily, you must be so exhausted all the time." I didn't get his point right away, not for a long time. Eventually, he helped me understand that not only am I not actually always right, but even if I was, it doesn't matter. It might never matter. This made all the difference in my desperation to learn how to fix a messed-up work culture from the inside. This was also the beginning of my journey of becoming willing to listen to other people… sometimes.

Lynett Kelly is someone who has consistently set an example for me of a leader who understands that if you invest in your employees, you don't have to worry about profits or the bottom line. Lynett, you are one of my greatest teachers of how to express gratitude. To me, you are now and have always been an example of perseverance, dedication, sacrifice, loyalty, the value of education, and what it really means to trust someone and to lose that. You continue to amaze me, and so do your children. I hope you can see all your successes the way I see them.

(Sidebar: Lynett also helped me begin to truly understand racism, and I'm so grateful to her for that. I will share what she taught me whenever I can do it peacefully.)

Lynett was my boss at this medical clinic that I worked at for several years in the mid-2000s. When I worked for Lynett, I had no experience in the medical world or working in an office. The starting pay then was $10/hour, and that was pretty good; they gave you another dollar when you made it through the first 90 days. Lynett's energy and commitment to high-quality staff inspired me to try harder and try to be better every day. She left, as the young and great ones do, on to bigger things as they grow and build on their careers and lives. I craved more instruction/guidance/training on how to motivate people and manage them. I looked to the internets, and they led me to many books. I read these books feverishly because I get excited when learning about how people are motivated and what makes us happy. That study led me to this work, studying/questioning/sharing as much as I can about building connections because relationships are everything.

Elemental Consulting was born from the idea that the simplest answer is usually the right answer. Is that one from some famous scientist? Pretty sure. Oh my word, are you kidding me? This one belongs to Occam's razor; you go ahead and Google that one – I just did. The idea is that the fundamentals are where we should focus our efforts and energy. The elements of the situation need to be examined. Elemental Consulting teaches that the building blocks for developing and sustaining a happy/healthy workforce culture are the same no matter what type of human conflict. These simple concepts require courage, commitment, and follow-through. The building blocks are consistency, honesty, trust, risk, and perseverance. As a consultant, I can provide you and your team with a customized training plan based on material that you can choose, or I can guide you in choosing the appropriate training subject matter after we have a realistic discussion about goals and the best use of everyone's time.

If you have a book you've been meaning to read and would love training in the topic, get in touch, and I'll happily make time to read it, digest it, and present a condensed version of it at the training venue that suits you (or I'll tell you it's crap and make another recommendation). You might be looking for someone for your employee engagement activity or a yearly conference where people can get new education to maintain professional licensure. You might be looking for intensive leadership workshops style training, direct support staff skills and soft skills training, or even leadership skills for all and team building that is not going to make people roll their eyes. Elemental Consulting is excited to help you start and keep on building healthy relationships at work.

Chapter 2: Relationships Are Everything

The Distance between Forgiveness and Condemnation

How do you find yourself a dog trainer? You ask around. What about finding someone to fix the guest bathroom downstairs off the kitchen? You ask around. What about if you need to find a new person to help with taxes? You ask around. It's all over social media, people asking for recommendations for everything from pet products to medical advice. We don't open the Yellow Pages (search engines nowadays for you young whipper snappers); we ask our community for recommendations. Relationships are everything, everywhere. Like it or not, we need each other; life is better because we work together. Speaking of relationships, I can recommend a great dog trainer! (The dog training link is an easter egg on my website; if you mention this tidbit to me at a conference, I'll have a little special something for you.)

How do you feel about snap judgments? Trust your gut, or wait and do some more investigation/research on the question? Once, a certified nursing assistant (CNA) reported to me, as their supervisor, that they were disappointed with their coworker's performance. I assured them I would follow up, and so I did. I went to the young man and said as much; that the coworker had reported disappointment in his performance for xyz reasons. He was immediately repentant and reassured me it would improve from here on. I reported back to the complainant, but I knew something she didn't, and that was who the accused identity *actually* was, and she still didn't know. This was someone she liked, and I was interested to see how this would pan out. I told her, "So (*so and so*) said that they were very sorry about that (mistake) and they would do better moving forward." Her immediate response was nonverbal – a sharp intake of breath, open mouth, wide eyes, hand to chest, and then she exclaimed something like,

"Oh, if I had known it was (so and so), I would have never said anything at all!"

Pretend I'm leaning into you now, and I'm looking deep in your pupils… and I ask you about this… as I asked her, sincerely interested to know, what qualifies someone to have immediate grace or immediate condemnation? She, of course, was not prepared to have a deep conversation with her temporary supervisor at 8 o'clock in the morning.

I believe that the distance between the person who was immediately condemned and the person who was immediately forgiven is the relationship. Space for your reflections below:

____

____

____

____

What crime does someone have to commit to you or around you, for them to qualify for immediate condemnation? Is it a cheater in a romance relationship? The person who doesn't stop for the school bus when the lights were flashing? Drunk driving? Your lunch got stolen? What about gossip passed around about you? Are you like the person in the story, who immediately condemned the imagined foe for not measuring up to an expectation?

One day at my house, hubby was waiting for a friend to come and help out with hauling some things away. I was mildly surprised that hubby hadn't been reminding me about this plan throughout the week, ensuring I'd be around to help. When I realized the friend was around, I got up to help, and hubby's body language was odd. I went to start helping and was redirected and educated on what the priorities were. My knee jerk was to bristle and give contrary advice, and then get mad about not being included in the aforementioned plans and prioritization. As I took myself out of the activity, I reflected that hubby planned this whole event, and did not include me pretty much at all. I could then understand that he didn't want me to butt in to the activity at all. He probably didn't know how to approach it, hey lady back off… might have resulted in conflict…

This is an opportunity for me to see what my partner was hoping for and to adjust so that I could be there for him and with him in a supportive way. I could tell by the way he expressed himself that he was really firm in his priorities for the day but also very hopeful that I wouldn't notice or be offended that I wasn't involved if I did notice. This would also be an opportunity for me to be angry, build a resentment and be hurtful. I could have explained to him why his priorities are out of whack and directed a much more efficient project. That may or may not be true, but it's irrelevant. What I value is peace and strength, so since I happened to be aware that it was even happening, I was able to choose, to actually make a conscious choice to be peaceful, and redirect my thinking so that my feelings are peaceful and I behave peacefully. I don't mind patting myself on the back a little here and there, because I also was able to reflect that choosing to be peaceful feels like building on emotional resilience, so I can put a tick mark on the column for being on track with both of my declared values.

Let's imagine another example, you're hard at work and a team member comes up to you to offer some help. You ask if they saw the memo, the memo that has a change in protocol on it. The memo that you know you complained to the supervisor about and now there's a memo. The team member who came up to you received your question about the memo in a defensive stance, having expected to come into some negativity based on the rumors of your complaints circling around the team. Your coworker says yes, of course, they saw the memo. Then they tell you how it is your fault that the memo is out and if you and yours had done your jobs right, this wouldn't have happened. During their response (you just knew it was going to be a negative response) you receive *their* response from a defensive position. You hear and assume that *they* are intentionally causing offense in the way they communicate their response to you. You respond in kind. Now you are both raising your voices, and the tension is building.

How could this conflict have been avoided? Do you think it could it have been avoided? What would have helped? Where could the two employees have build understanding instead of resentment? What if instead of trying to prevent the conflict, we become adept at managing it when it happens, and expert at recovering from conflict anywhere?

Space for reflection:

____

____

____

____

____

____

What practices can we put in place that build habits of efficient recovery from conflict? How could this look at work or at home? Would it be different at all, if so, why?

____

____

____

____

____

____

In order to build practices that promote quick and constructive conflict recovery we need to understand where things stand now, what barriers are in place, and how we will measure success. At my house we have a culture of discussion post conflict, when we are not feeling emotional. This distance between discussion and conflict is useful in our relationship, in order to identify triggers and/or make amends. My hubby needs to charge through conflict and get to the resolution and closure asap. I prefer space and time, so I don't behave in a way I'll have to apologize for later. When we are not feeing all up in our emotions, we discuss strategy and predictable barriers… but not in that language. Part of our amends process is to try to plan for the next time we are triggered so we behave more in line with our values.

We will always have conflict, every day that we are humans who interact with other humans no matter what the environment is like or where it happens to be. Preventing conflict is a wonderful idea, but it is not a very practical idea. One human does not have the power to prevent another human from behaving in any particular way. We cannot prevent each other from having any particular feelings or thoughts or even actions. We can choose to stay, and be there for each other, while in conflict. We can choose to stay and try to understand each other. We can stay and sit together, even in disagreement, trying peacefully to work through it. My hubby doesn't need me to tell him why he is or isn't ___(fill in the blank)___. For example, he doesn't need me to say:

You're not stupid, it's ok.

You just need to put it in the same place every time, simple!

Stop being mad at yourself!

It might be helpful for me to sit, wait, be curious and patient, and listen. That's hard for me. I want to direct, advise, solve, push, fix, suggest, and be in charge. I have observed that if I can be spiritually well enough to recognize it is happening, I can remember my old mantra, 'shut up Emily, shut up Emily, shut up Emily'. Instead I can ask him what he needs, taking an attitude of curiosity (thank you to Brene Brown for that one) instead of having decided the diagnosis, prognosis and treatment of whatever I have perceived the problem at hand to be.

Chapter 3. What Are the Barriers to Building Healthy Relationships At Work?

I get excited about this one; let's name some language that limits our thinking and smash it. How about seniority as an employee benefit? How about shame in the workplace? What stops you from developing healthy and constructive relationships at work? What does a healthy relationship at work look like, and what is the evidence? Why are we even discussing this? Room for some notes below. Remember to dig a little deeper:

____

____

____

____

____

____

Over the years, Baby Boomers and Gen Xers have worked hard (just ask us) at building a work force that gets things done. No time for nonsense; let's get things done. We have asked our workers to be non-human, if possible. Take only the allotted breaks, leave your problems at the door, and you can pick them up when you leave. However, it turns out that humans are best at being human, and the non-human stuff doesn't really work well for long-term healthy workforce cultures.

I have found that unhealthy work relationships are typically hard to spot from the inside. We get used to observing the behavior and ignore it or become desensitized to it. Ask an outsider to observe the team and then come report their suspicions about unhealthy relationships and culture. An unhealthy relationship at work might look something like this:

Two parties are the same gender. One is a manager-level employee, while the other is an hourly employee in the same department. They have both been at this company for ten-plus years and have been close friends along the way. They hang out together outside of work and discuss work outside of work through the lens of a social acquaintance and not leadership. One tends to be a bit of a bully; the other one has a new manager who is teaching the team to have a constructive culture and focuses on positive language and reinforcement/teaching. Occasionally, one of them is critical in a sarcastic way and sometimes jokes in public spaces about sensitive issues in their personal lives.

What makes you cringe about that? Can you point out things that are inappropriate? Room for notes here:

____

____

____

____

____

Other examples might look like:

Family members who have never been able to cooperate or communicate effectively. They are also in the upper-level leadership of the company and make most of the decisions about day-to-day operations, payroll/finance, and spending. They also have inappropriate and unprofessional discussions in front of staff and customers.

Someone who chronically seeks out opportunities to "stir the pot" of gossip or intense energy, and that is sort of their "role" on the team. This person might spend too much time focused on their coworkers' performance, attendance, or personal life and share information far and wide.

In all these examples, we can find a common thread: The culture has accepted this behavior, and it has been going on long enough that only new people notice it. New people tend to try assimilating quickly and are unlikely to rock the boat that they just started working on. The behavior is accepted by the majority of people and it is taken for granted that it will not change, so we just shut it off from our perception, like background music.

How can we bring about meaningful and sustainable change? I apologize in advance for this answer because having appropriate education (appropriate training) and consistent and meaningful *boundaries* is the key to success here. Brene Brown has excellent research and writing on boundaries, which I highly recommend.

What is it that stops the employee from doing the right thing all the time? When does the employee decide it doesn't matter? Why do some supervisors avoid these behavior correction discussions? What is it that *you* avoid facing in the human relation world? What is it that *you* are terrified someone will ask *you* to do, with all this "human relation" stuff? This is a good place to spend some time exploring, but maybe bring a friend. We often find our own character defects while seeking to further our understanding of other people's character defects, so brace yourself. Room for you to take notes on your own reflections.

Shame is often a significant barrier to building meaningful connections with other humans. Some interactions at some time in the past somehow taught you that you shouldn't just say what you want. That's too pushy, or needy, or egotistical, or inappropriate, or undeserved; you have to manipulate the world around you to be safe to say what you want. What is it that stops you from answering a question in a group of people? What is it that makes you dread to answer the phone? What is it that prevents you from telling someone if you are having a bad day instead of holding it in when they ask you how you are doing? Don't cheat yourself here; dig deep:

I suspect that a large part of the reasons we do the things we do is because of our inability or unwillingness to have honest discussions with each other socially. We do not even have honest dialogues with ourselves. We do not typically say to ourselves the counsel we share with others when they struggle. We tell ourselves we need to hide our problems, that no one would understand, and if they *really* knew you, they wouldn't like you. We protect our soft spots from the outside world, and our feelings are often those soft spots.

Have you ever had the "What's for Dinner" fight? I talked to a friend about this one, and she told me that in their house, this conflict recurs, and it happens because she doesn't want to cook. She told me, "I usually… ok, I almost never want to cook. It's just so much work."

I asked her, "Can you tell me why you don't just say to him, *please don't ask me to cook tonight; it's too much work, let's do this instead?"*

She explained that she is afraid he will really want her to cook and that, eventually, they will order out, but she desperately wishes they could cut out the recurring conflict.

At our house, the struggle is to say what is *actually* going on. My darling might say to me,

"What do you want to do tonight?"

He is attempting to avoid saying: What's for dinner? Because that question instigates hostility. What he really is trying to say is: *Please want what I want, but I can't ask for what I want because I just can't...* The most recent round of the "What are we doing for dinner" fight was an interesting one. Eventually, we made it through. Earlier in the afternoon, he had been listing off to me what his day entailed, and it was a long list of going here and there and doing this and that. What I missed was that he felt that his day had been extraordinarily difficult and also successful. He was hoping I would share in that celebration of hard work and success with him but was not able to ask for that. Instead, he listed the things he did and expected a specific response, which I did not give (and rarely do). He was able to tell me at one point that he had made it *very clear to me earlier...* This clued me in and helped me talk about it with him because I remembered that he had pointedly and repeatedly listed his accomplished tasks for the day. If he believed his need was obvious, then I must be deliberately not doing it. We both agreed that was probably not true. I asked him, "So if *that* is true, I'm asking you to tell me what you need, can you try?" and if we are both spiritually… like… well enough, then we get through that together. If we aren't, then it takes us longer to come back to the baseline.

We want people to see and know what we want so we don't have to be vulnerable to ask for it. This is not constructive for any relationship in any setting. There is a popular idea that a perfect romantic partner would be able to tell when we need a hug, drink, snack, sex, affection, or validation and give it to us freely without having to ask for any of those things. This is silly; this is a way to stay unhappy in the relationship and to put all the ownership on the other person. This idea that I don't want if I have to ask for it is absurd.

Why is it so difficult for us to ask for what we want/need? What if we instead tried to focus on becoming this ideal romantic partner instead of trying to find someone who doesn't exist?

If I say to my sweetie, *"No, I'm fine,"* but I'm not fine; this is an opportunity to be real with myself and real with my sweetie. I don't expect my sweetie to know what I'm upset about without me telling them. This is unclear and unkind (that is from Brene Brown). For me, at home, I need time before I can figure out what is actually bothering me so I can participate in the discussion (or fight, whatever you want to call it). Instead of saying the less true words above, *"No, I'm fine,"* I could say to sweetie, "I'm not ok, but I need time before I can talk about this. Can you give me 15 minutes with myself? And then I'll be ready to talk."

The trick is being honest with ourselves first. We need to try to say what we mean. If we can analyze conflict when we are not feeling emotional, we might be able to find the trigger and name it so we have better tools the next time the trigger is set off. Super sexy relationship advice, right?

Here is another example you might be able to relate to about being honest with yourself in order to be honest with others. Let's say you're mad at your boss. They forgot to do something they said they would do for you. They let you down, and this time, it was just extra… whatever. It hurts. The words I tell myself might sound like this:

"What the eff. WHAT THE EFF. Sighhhhhhhhhhhhhh. Fine, fine. Yup. Ok, ok. FINE."

Angry words that aren't really appropriate to type here in this book because my mom will read it for sure, and I don't want her to read those words in my voice.

Hulk smash!

If I were more honest with myself, it might sound more like this:

"I'm scared I'm not as important as I thought I was here."

"I'm scared that I might not understand my role like I thought I did."

"What is wrong with me? Did I mess this up????...."

"This makes me feel like my job isn't as secure as I thought it was. And maybe I can't trust my boss either, and that is disappointing."

Then, the boss says to you, "Hey, are you ok? You don't look like yourself today."

You *could* say something like,

"You know what? My feelings are hurt and I'm struggling to deal with it. You forgot to do that thing you said you would take care of. It makes me feel like you don't care about the work I do. I feel silly for pouring my heart into this project right now. How could you forget that?"

But instead, you say something like,

"Oh, I'm fine. I haven't had any caffeine yet this morning."

Chapter 4: Where Do We Even Start?

Well, what do you *really* want? I want to have the things I value. How do I *know* what I value, and how can I tell that person/place/thing is the thing that I *value*? *H*ow do I know what I want? Write down your initial thoughts about what you value here.

____
____
____
____
____
____

I had to spend some time digging around inside and outside of myself to figure out just what that was. Lots and lots of books about leadership teach us that we need to define what we value. This is important for you to understand your goals and where you're headed. I was talking to one of my teachers, M. Anne Day, and she was teaching me about how she learned that when you don't have any defined goals to work toward, it is like being in a boat with no oars. It's a great boat; you're comfortable, and you're safe, but you're just not going anywhere. Anne has taught me a great many things, but this is one of my favorites. Humans are happier when they are working toward something. So, if we should be working toward something, we'd better figure out what is important to us.

I don't like to waste time. Lucky for us, many people have written and researched this idea. Brene Brown has a whole giant list of words in her Dare to Lead book that you can use to help you define your values. I found this list to be pretty debilitating. I couldn't connect to the words on the page (imagine I'm making a face with my mouth twisted up to the side in thought). How. Do. I. Choose. Words. To. Represent. My. Values? This took me a lot of time and many, many conversations with people around me. I rely on my community to help me understand the world.

I have landed on two values. I know, I know, she said to pick three. You'll just have to live with it. I'm very nontraditional (wink). Peace and strength are my values. Peace in all things and in all ways is what I desire deep down inside. I'm talking blanket out of the dryer cozy kind of peace. I strive to recover peace quickly when it is disturbed. I recognize that my peace is only disturbed by myself or under my consent/participation. I long to be slow to anger and quick to forgive. I desire to forget all cutting and sharp words from my vocabulary and my heart. I pray to conquer sarcasm and abolish it from my spirit all together. I strive to express myself in the most peaceful, honest, kind, and gentle ways (this will be a lifelong challenge for me).

Strength refers to physical, intellectual, spiritual, and emotional strength. To me, this is evidenced by resilience, drive, and the pursuit of happiness. I have committed to continue to choose to reach for good physical health through consistent, mostly good nutrition most of the time. This year, one of my goals is to build consistent exercise into my routine. I have applied for a leadership training course from this year to next, and I'm looking forward to building my skills and helping our team strengthen the community further. I am also working toward an HR certification that will open doors for me to bring information to you in your workplace. I am also working on building a better connection between my mind and body. I often ignore many signals from my body, can you relate? It sometimes looks like this:

I'm not hungry

I don't have to pee

It can wait... no, really, I can wait. I'm good at waiting.

Waiting gives me more time to ignore what my body is trying to tell me. This is that dishonesty with self I keep talking about. I'm not real with myself if I deny hunger or the need to relieve my bladder. If I'm going to be able to define what I really want, I need to be real with myself. I work to acknowledge when my body needs something, even if I can't meet the need right away. I'm trying to stop ignoring my body when it wants my attention. I continue to strive to be brave in seeking to develop strength and/or the capacity for increased strength.

What do you want?

____

____

____

____

What do you value?

Once we have a better understanding of what we *actually* want, let's take stock of what we've got. Some of my teachers along the way have given me the following advice: *Make sure you inventory the good stuff, too*. Looking at your workplace or your team of staff, where do things stand now, and how can you tell? At your workplace, what is the measure of success in the culture? Is the measure that there is lots of social engagement outside of work? Is it great attendance or great retention? Great income projections for the upcoming year? If you can identify the measure of success, it'll help provide a way to measure progress along the way, and you'll have a destination to plug into your "GPS." That analogy comes from the Hollaway Group here in Maine.

I challenge you to put together a handful of people who will tell you the truth, although, fair warning: this is not for the faint of heart. Ask those people who are not afraid to tell you the truth to tell you about the things others *are* afraid to tell you. Reach for growth in whatever area you hope people never look at too closely. It's the area that you know you need to do better in, yet you are afraid to ask for help for whatever reason. There might (probably is) even be some shame attached to it.

Now that we have a better idea of where we stand and where we want to go, it's time to make a plan of how to get there, like a road map. You might not believe this, but I used to have to go on to the internet through a *dial-up* modem; wait… for a machine to convert the dialing to an internet address… to a digital signal… and then jump to turn down the volume knob with my **bare hand**, when the terrible internet handshake sound came on that underlined the discord of digital and analog… Then, I would look up an address and *write* down the steps with a tool you pick up in your hand and use it to make marks on paper. There would be a human navigator in the vehicle, who was responsible for managing the steps. That's a lot of labor compared to how things are now when you need to get from here to there. Defining where we are now is critical to be able to make a map of where we are headed. What is the first thing you do when you look at a map? I always look for where I am represented on the map. I need to get my bearings to understand the map itself. I know you'll be disappointed in me here, but there's no easy formula for the map. This part is completely relative to *your* priorities at *your* workplace. The priorities for intervention at my workplace will inevitably be different than the priorities at yours.

Start out by making a clear statement about what the objective is. For me, this is a slow process, and I tend to redesign it several times as I go along. Some examples of a starter thought might be:

I need my staff to stop fighting.

I need my staff to show up.

I need my boss to be more reliable.

I'm afraid I can't offer the staff the money they are demanding.

I don't know how to motivate these people.

I don't know where to start to have a healthy social/professional culture at work.

This is too big to face; things will never change. I'm the only one thinking this.

With these first thoughts, we can glean clearer, objective information by developing ideas and insights and translating those into a goal that is a response to the highest priorities for intervention.

If you say to me, "I need my staff to stop fighting," I'm going to ask you, "How do you know?" Let's gather some objective data and see what that tells us. Through this process, we will work together to form a clear objective, and from that, we can design a path. A broad example of a problem statement might be: staff surveys show that 75% of the staff feel that they do not have an avenue to express complaints at work. Your objective might shape up to be something like this: by January 1, 2026, improvement of the surveyed staff complaint will be evidenced by (reduced percentage) of (same measure) on staff survey. You can fancy it up in your professional jargon later. For now, focus on meaningful interventions and focus on the goal.

Meet with the team, debrief from the planning stages and make sure everyone is on the same page with the objective moving forward. If not, spend more time here until you have a united group of people working toward the same goal; this is worth the extra time. Look for barriers to understanding in the group as you work toward unity. You may uncover uncommon language, meaning that you use the same words, but they mean different things, relatively speaking. This is often the trigger of missed communication. Common language is crucial to cooperation. If one person defines the word "short" to mean five minutes and another person means five days, that is going to lead to problems.

Now, it's time to plan the execution of the new strategies. It's likely that through the early stages of this process, you have already started to implement change. It often happens that way: it's on your mind, you discuss it with other people, and then your own behavior and language change. You notice things a little differently; it's happening spontaneously because you and the team are putting energy into it, and you're focused on solutions, not problems.

That all sounds good, but this is the part where people fall off track. We've had some great ideas, but now what? I bet you've experienced this before. You have a great idea to improve some part of your life. Say it's weight loss or learning a new musical instrument. You've discovered a new thing that changed your mindset, and you are ready to reach this new goal. You do a little Googling and even tell your closest couple of friends about your plan. You buy a new (whatever you need) for your exciting plan (workout clothes and a new water jug or a new guitar and strings and stand). You are ready and MOTIVATED.

And then… somewhere in the first or second stages of work, the whole thing falls apart. Shawn Achor writes about reducing the activation energy reflecting on barriers to success. Shawn was prepared to achieve a goal but what he found was that he would not even consider the pursuit of the goal unless it was easier than not pursuing the goal. We don't change unless it is easier to change than it is to stay the same. I like to describe it like this: we won't do anything about the dishes until it's easier to do something with them than it is to leave them there any longer. Everyone's path to success is different; you might wash the dishes, where I might throw them away and get paper plates, and someone else might burn the whole house down.

Shawn learned that he needed to go further to set himself up for success when he wanted to learn how to play the guitar and, at the same time, make a good habit of practicing daily. He had a plan, and he was prepared with tools like a calendar to mark progress and have visual reminders. He gave himself 30 days but did not follow through with his plan. The guitar was way down the hall in the closet, and that was just too much work compared to sitting down and picking up the remote control for the TV. At the end of the 30-day plan, Shawn found he had not learned to play the guitar. He decided to make it easier. Shawn took the guitar out of the closet and put it in the TV room. He took the remote control for the TV, removed the batteries, and put them in a drawer and the remote control in another drawer. Now, it would be easier for him to work on the guitar than it would be to sit down and watch TV. Shawn talks about this in terms of activation energy. Reduce the activation energy if you want to increase your likeliness of success. All this to say, you must plan to be prepared and then be willing to plan again when things don't go as planned. This is where most people stop, but this is where the work happens.

We have got to get to work and keep at it. We can't approach the health of our workforce culture (or office or home) while thinking of it as a one-time thing that just needs to be treated, and then it will go away. As long as your workplace has humans in it, you will have culture problems. Humans are just everywhere. Let's approach the plan of execution as a long-term plan. This reminds me of Shawn Achor's writing, where he teaches how he learned that having a different perspective is key. This plan should be considered a living document without an expiration date. Break it down into small goals and focus on small and meaningful interventions that happen consistently and every single day. Oh, that's Shawn again; he says that when a problem looks too big, we have to choose to see it differently. I say to myself and others, "Make it make sense." Of course, we *can* do this, but where do we *start*? Look to the list of starter ideas we made earlier if you need to get your juices flowing.

What is a problem that feels too big to face? It doesn't have to be at work; it could be outside of work.

____

____

____

____

____

____

Break your plan down into small goals and focus on small and meaningful interventions. That sounds good, but how? Let's say the goal is to reduce the percentage of unhappy employees in that survey from before. That sentence is too big to start making an action plan. What can we do every day to move closer to the goal? What can we start working with to get closer to the goal? Where is the biggest need? What is the priority? These types of questions will help you build out your plan for execution.

We often tell ourselves that we'll be happy when ___________ (fill in the blank). We believe that happiness is just out of reach and that if we just do the one right thing, we'll finally have it! Easy street, smooth sailing, downhill from here. Won't that be nice? When we finally figure out what that one thing is that will make us successful and then, *then* we can be happy. When I get that job, that relationship, that paycheck, that degree, finish this class, buy that car, become a homeowner, you get the picture. I have good news; you don't have to wait anymore. You can go ahead and pursue happiness now. Shawn Achor's research shows that we become successful as we pursue happiness and not the other way around. Doesn't that just beat all? I love the way he defines happiness, too, stating that happiness is the condition we are in when we are reaching out for our potential. I'm reaching out to become willing to change in the first place before I can even begin to consider changing.

____

____

____

____

____

____

The thing that I hope you hear in these pages is that consistency is the most important ingredient. In order to bring sustainable change to the culture, it must evolve into a spontaneous practice, and the management *must* implement a plan to continue to support the changes and nurture the culture in order for it to continue to grow and develop and not be consumed by weeds. If I ignore this plant, we can predict, based on lots of research about plant care, that the plant's potential to bear fruit will exceed our expectations when our participation doesn't limit the plant's potential. If I give it the things it needs and then also provide opportunities for it to thrive, I will have a better plant. If I continue to regularly maintain this health and promote further development and growth, this is what will determine the success of my garden (or workforce team, whichever works best for you. How did we end up in a garden analogy?). Don't forget, we need to be able to measure the fruit of our labors, too. The staff that I have the privilege of serving as a leader will always have more success and more capacity for success if I don't get in their way. My own thinking limits their success if I'm not careful.

Regarding consistency and sustainable change, typically, we'll see a new staff morale and wellness initiative rolled out. Something like a big 5k event, and there's all this hype and promotion around the 5k. Great turnout at the race, excellent PR opportunities, and social media posting is happening. About one year out, there is a review of the goals in a board meeting, and someone asks how the big 5k race impacted the staff morale/wellness. And then everyone at the table realizes that the debrief meeting we planned to have in order to prepare for the next big event never even got scheduled.

How can we manifest a sustainable priority shift focused on the maintenance of the improved condition once the newness of the initiative has worn off? The principles are the same for success here as anywhere else. Name the goal, name the distance from the goal to where you are now, then make a plan. Start the post-project planning now as well; set a date for the debrief meeting and another date within four weeks after that to plan how to execute the post-project planning. Planning needs to include how to execute or roll out the new project/initiative, divvy up who on the team is responsible for what sections and how to measure that success.

Decide what the benchmarks are and where they belong on your path to success, and map it out on your calendars as well, setting up checkpoints along the way for accountability and clarity of common language. Decide how the team will tell each other when a change is needed, *how* Jane will tell Joe that he is falling behind on his timeline and this could compromise the success of the whole team. Plan out this conflict resolution when emotions are relaxed, and invite and facilitate honest conversation about how to approach tension and potential for resentment. Have an entirely separate meeting for this culture building if possible. Prepare the team for this discussion with the agenda or an outline or assignment. Time will be wasted if they aren't prepared for the discussion. Ask them to come prepared to discuss how they would like to be informed when they need to change behavior, that they are wrong, or that the team needs more from them. Give the team language to use, such as, *I have something hard to talk about. Are you ready now, or do you need more time?*

When there has been an ongoing conflict that just won't go away, it can be all but impossible to inject the resolution peacefully and without any employee terminations. Suggestions for approach: the leader observes a time when emotions are baseline with the crew and takes the opportunity to discuss the conflict and hash out potential solutions. Set a culture together, meaning decide, discuss, and negotiate how you will behave during the discussion and how to self-correct if the behavior is out of line with the agreed-upon culture. Approach this meeting with curiosity so that you don't limit their work with that bias/nonverbal communication that would come from your bias. If you can't do that for the team, find someone else to; you will not be useful.

We can plan interventions for predictable conflicts; that is my favorite thing about them. We will make better choices when emotions are running hot if we've already talked it out. I bet you know what I'm going to say: this strategy has a meaningful impact on all human relationships, in my experience.

Consider the 'What's for Dinner' fight we mentioned earlier. If it's predictable, we should be able to do something about it. Many people have great ideas about how to prevent this conflict. Some people suggest delegating specific nights to specific people to manage. Someone suggested a game where people make novelty items to help manage this decision. You can roll a die, and whatever it lands on is what you agree to do for dinner. I'm tempted to say, can't we just fend for ourselves? I don't have, and never really have had, a culture of social time around meals at home. I don't think that games and assignments will resolve anything, as well as digging into the issue at hand. The issue at hand seems to me that we won't or can't make ourselves vulnerable to say what we want for whatever reason.

Brene Brown's book about shame, I Thought It Was Just Me. (but it isn't), has several examples with a raw discussion about why we don't make ourselves vulnerable. She finds that there are common threads and this powerful way to see how we make decisions out of fear and scarcity because of our shame. This is how we cope with our shame. I highly recommend this book, but I recommend reading it with a buddy to help process complicated, icky-feeling stuff. Brace yourself; we are going to dig into some of my shame stories.

(Mom, I'm going to tell this story, but I do not approve of you using this to make yourself feel more mom guilt, which is what she says is her right. I don't argue with my momma.)

I was in high school at the time and was starting to get leaner, coming out of my puffy/fluffy middle school years. I remember trying on this vest that my mother had worn. I was so envious of my mom's grown-up body and wanted my body to flippin cooperate; her clothes did not make my body look like her body. This vest was so pretty, with fall colors, and the threads had a bit of a shine on them; it was black with autumn leaves embroidered on it. I tried it on, and Mom came in the room, beamed at me, and said it would look so great in five more pounds! I was instantly deflated, but my mother's face was joyful, so I told myself the feeling was wrong and put it away. This is what my memory tells me; I know fully well that my mother was praising me at that moment. Her own bias and feelings about weight colored that praise, and I received it as shame for not being thin enough or looking right enough in this clothing.

Once, we found an old family photo that included my older brother. It was a professional photo, and we only had those done a couple of times with the family, maybe twice. I complained to Mom about how I looked in the photo, and she counseled me not to smile so big that it made my eyes close in the photo and made my face look chubby.

When I was in elementary school, maybe second grade, my

family and I were practicing Jehovah's Witnesses. If you don't already know, faith does not participate in world American cultural or religious holidays in any way. Public schools run on the holiday calendar, you know what I mean? All the events and curriculum are planned to include and celebrate all those days. These days, I think they even include many other countries and cultures in their celebrations, but that wouldn't have benefited me. We were not allowed to participate. One winter, I was told we were making Christmas decorations to take home. The teacher told me not to worry that she had non-Christmas colors for me to work with and was sure I'd be able to participate instead of sitting quietly and watching everyone else make Christmas decorations. I chose blue and green and began working on my project; I chose a bird. The teacher came around and told me how green and blue do **not** go together, and I might want to start again. I was already full of shame when she came.

In middle school, I was finally invited to a sleepover, like a real one. Not my cousins or church friends, but like where these 'real' kids went to have fun and do things like I saw on TV, like on the Cosby show. That night, they let me know in slight and subtle ways that I was the joke at the party. I didn't really let it sink in or believe it. I wanted to tell the voice in my head; there was no way that they were laughing at me, no way they were joking about my clothes and what was in my bag. The next day, when I went to school in that space where kids hung out before it was time to go into the bell, they called me over to the steps where the cool kids hung out and very publicly gave me back my underwear they had taken from my bag at the sleepover.

Shame is powerful. Shame stops me from being open and honest with others, often. How about you?

Chapter 5: Keep it Going

No human can *force* any other human to do anything at all. I really believe that, but I can feel some of you having a familiar twitch to argue with that sentence. There is a scene in the movie *Dances with Wolves* where one of the characters tells another something to that effect, and it stuck with me all these years. I remember it well because I was a leader in my family and struggled to keep the kids in line. My parents split up and remarried, and our group of siblings was frequently unsupervised. I'm naturally pretty bossy (yeah, yeah) and, as such, led the unruly group of budding juvenile delinquents. I struggled to keep these savages from bloodying each other. Rules and laws do not limit or predict behavior, or our jails would be empty. Rules and laws can predict cost, but that is a talk for another book. Motivation comes from within; behavior correction does, too. When that movie told me that no one can make anyone do anything, it stuck with me and gave me a new question. What does make people do things?

Did I already tell you my two theories? The first is that relationships are everything. The second is that my thinking drives my feelings, which drives my actions, so if my behavior needs correction, I should start by fixing my thinking. I believe the thinking>feeling>acting thing comes from Brene Brown's <u>Dare To</u> series. If I got that wrong, feel free to correct me.

David Marquet talks about how he learned that it is the responsibility of leadership to provide opportunities for each member of the team to choose to put in the work to succeed in his book Turn the Ship Around. The humans themselves must take responsibility for the outcome of their labor. I have searched and searched for books that would tell me *how* to motivate people to *want* to be excellent, but there is no easy answer so far. It turns out nothing works as well as motivating ourselves. Nothing motivates us better than when we are encouraging those we love to succeed.

Back in the early 21st century (sigh), I was working as a trainer at a call center for an internet access company. I couldn't figure out, in my infinite wisdom of 22-ish years, just why people didn't *want* to try hard. I actually *wanted* to try hard, simply for the sake of being better than the next guy. I could not wrap my head around the idea that people didn't have a desire to reach for excellence, for the sake of achievement itself. I was sent out to the West Coast to the state of Washington for some branded customer service training. They used the HEART model. Please feel free to email me and tell me who I should thank for that; I couldn't find a trademark for it. Here is what I remember of it. Please be patient with me here as I'm sure this model has been adapted many times, and my memory is mostly made up of what I *want* to remember as the truth… as one does… so thank you for your fact-checking. I'm happy to do a press release or something to give out the proper thank yous as they may be owed.

H- hear and understand

E- expect the best

A- act with integrity

R- respect diversity

T- transcend yourself

This acronym is an excellent quick reference reminder of where our compass should be pointed for the pursuit of success in all our human-to-human encounters. As you consider how to start meeting with the team to flesh out the ideas and concerns you have, consider what your specific and personal objective is related to your leadership and your role on the team. I believe this will help you bring constructive energy to the team, and you are solely responsible for driving that kind of vibe on the team. Be there for them; if you don't believe that they can win, they won't. Believe that the team can win, and they will feel your belief in them. If you don't believe that they can, this is your starting point. Check your own side of the street if you don't believe the team can get the job done. Discuss the principles you are focused on improving with the team. Explain what you're hoping for, what you're scared of, and the purpose of building a healthy workforce culture; this gives the team some ownership in the outcome.

I had a "duh" moment not too long ago, and I'd like to share it with you. You remember that old story about how back, way back before we talked much about ethics and such… certainly before we had a whole HR department… ok, way back then, these psychologist-type people took these two groups of kids and presented them to some teachers. The researchers told the teachers that group A was a group of high performers, while group B was, unfortunately, a group of low performers, and you couldn't really expect much from them at all. Guess how things turned out? Yes! The ones who were in a room with a leader who thought they could perform at a high level did well. On the other hand, the ones who were in a room with a leader who expected poor results performed poorly.

The point of the study was that the kids were all the same. The only difference was how they were thought of; what people believed of them. My takeaway here is that how we treat people can be a barrier to or a springboard for their success. I realized one day that I had introduced one of my staff to someone with vocabulary words that implied all the characteristics about them that I didn't really celebrate. As soon as I realized it, I changed it. (It took more than two years, in case you're wondering how long it took me.) I began to use vocabulary that implied potential, expertise, and excellence in a loud and public way. You can imagine this has manifested some positive change in that person and the team culture.

As you approach the team, check your compass and make sure you are looking and expecting a successful team, you'll be much more likely to find one. Start the discussion about your own culture on this team and design the rules of discussion together. Decide, take a deep breath, and start.

Chapter 6: Full Disclosure

I had an extreme childhood. The details don't really matter; trauma is trauma, and it's not helpful to compare. I loved roller-skating (not at Happy Wheels), talking on the phone all night, listening to Janet Jackson, Jurassic 5, Guns n Roses, and Sebastian Bach. I joined the US Air Force almost immediately out of high school and landed in Colorado Springs working at the 721st Communications Squadron for Space Command, inside of Cheyenne Mountain Air Force Base. I worked hard to develop my drinking habits, level up, level up, level up. I landed in 12-step peer support recovery and therapy in the spring of 2001 at the age of 24. The good stuff didn't really take until around 2005 when my community taught me about just how dishonest I was and how to take direction. That changed my life and is the challenge of my life.

It's only fair to tell those of you who don't already see/hear the recovery language in my vernacular that when I reflect on my adult life, it is through this lens. I found intense relief from the madness in peer support recovery meetings. And I'll have you know that I also detest 12-step peer recovery meetings. The bummer is that it is all true, and it makes me roll my eyes that it is real and true. The sayings are true; all corny sayings are true. Sigggggghhhhh.

Brene Brown writes about her experiences with recovery, trauma, shame, and empathy. She uses language that is easy for me to connect to and that always impresses me. Verbal/written communication can be such a struggle for me and so many of us.

While I studied over the last year or so, I was focused on the language/concept that Brene writes about, that shame drives disconnection. Empathy is the antidote to shame. You could also say shame drives addiction. Rearrange those words again to read empathy is the antidote to addiction. Brene says that shame itself is shameful to even discuss verbally, among civilized company. That is such a strong image to me, and significant. You know me; I get excited about challenging old ideas and vocabulary if it will bring more understanding and opportunity.

My full-time work is nursing in a residential facility in Bangor, Maine. Our workplace is one of the happiest places on Earth, most of the time. It's full of humans, so we have ups and downs. My primary work there is to take very good care of our CNAs. My part-time work is with Home Health and Hospice patients here locally in Maine. This work is a dream for me. For when I am doing hospice work, I can see that there is evidence of a higher purpose in life.

My tertiary work is this work, helping people build relationships and leverage humanness to our advantage instead of trying to extinguish it or somehow exist by being less human at work. I also volunteer through my faith community and in the substance abuse community locally. I love to roller skate but am too old to take those kinds of risks these days, ha! I love to make art because it gives my spirit relief to manipulate things with my hands into a sense of organization or pleasure. I find this relief through drawing, painting, jewelry making, sculpting, writing, singing, and, most recently, cooking! I learned how to cook this year, and it has been wonderful.

I'm not always happy, but people do describe me that way. I tend to expect the best from people and situations. I expect to win or at least to do well. I plan to make new friends and be pleasant and hopeful. I choose to believe that people are essentially good, and we all want the same things (Maslow's basement as my teacher Sheilagh refers to it): food/shelter/safety, but beyond that, we also need to feel welcome, useful, competent and beyond that, appreciated, valued, validated, and encouraged. Beyond that, opportunities to grow and transcend yourself (see the HEART model). It is rare that someone is just looking for ways to be mean/hurtful/insensitive/unfriendly, etc. It's just that we are typically tuned in to ourselves and what we need, see, think, and feel. Human responses are relative to what is happening with them and rarely what is happening with you/me.

For example, my darling husband and I are preparing to take the dogs out somewhere. I am preparing things to depart; where is my bag, my cup, etc? Tending to the doggos to make sure they are ready to leave, I find myself preparing to ask my husband if he knows where the dog's collar is. What is remarkable to me is that I noticed I was preparing to ask him. I realized I expected the question to upset him. I remember when we had a big fight one day after I had asked about the dog's leash. We were preparing to leave to go to a park. I asked about the leash; he went into the garage for several minutes. When he came back, he was visibly upset. I later learned that he had been beating himself up for not ever putting things away and telling himself how stupid he was for not doing better, and on and on. So, when he came back into the room, he was snappy, and his tone and words were unkind and impatient. That turned into a big fight out in public and in the car. Before we got home, we had reconciled in peace that we did not understand each other that day. Another day, we were able to discuss it again and understand that the trigger had come with the feeling of not being good enough to even put the leash away. So, I was preparing to ask him about the dog collar. I said gently, "Do you happen to know where the dog's collar is?" It does, in fact, lead to some conflict, but we were able to resolve it in minutes this time, resulting in a peaceful exchange, with hugs and kisses and an enjoyable outing with our doggos.

He wasn't upset because I asked about the leash or the collar. He responded through the lens of what was happening to him at that time. He looked through a different lens than I did. If I ask myself what I can do differently to prevent future conflict, there might not be a great answer. I'm not going to avoid asking the question, but I'm going to be prepared to be peaceful and expect the best as I approach predictable conflict. This is what I think of as an efficient recovery from conflict.

If my happiness was conditional upon my husband's happiness or wellness or his interventions, then I just want to be unhappy because that is not going to work. If I depend on my work to make me happy, my boss to make me happy, or someone else to do something to make me happy, it's not likely that I'll find it. If I find myself angry and in a conflict with someone or something, I might say something like, "They shouldn't have poked the bear," in reference to me losing my temper. This puts all the responsibility for my actions on the other person as if they have the power to make me lose my temper or behave badly. If someone stomps on my toe and my response is to punch them in the nose… that is still on me. You didn't make me punch you in the nose; it is a response that is relative to whatever is going on with me. If I am angry about the toe stomping, that is not because my toe got stomped; it is because of whatever is happening to me. I'm probably hungry, if I'm honest. Essentially, it boils down to what I learned in the halls of 12-step peer recovery: whenever I am disturbed, the problem is with me.

Chapter 7: Wrap it Up Already

I Do So Love the Sound of My Own Voice... Don't You?

It's so tempting to just buy into the nice things people say about me after a public appearance. It's so inviting to just get up on stage and say... TA DAAAA!!! (Picture Bette Midler or someone who is just electric on stage and beams in the delight of the audience.) The work I want to do is to be there for you. I want you to think of me when you need help. In order for me to keep my ego in check, I have to focus on the service part of this work. It helps tremendously to have people around who will tell me the truth. They will tell me when I'm behaving in a way that is out of line with what they perceive my values to be. The ideas I share here with you, are not my own but what has been taught to me so generously, painfully, or painstakingly. I am committed to creating opportunities for learning and making information about building connections as accessible to as many people as I can.

The secret to happiness is simple: build a habit of looking after people around you. You can build these habits like any other, make a plan, plan to execute the plan, execute the plan and kick off your post plan debrief…even if the whole team is just you. I decided when leaving a long time job, that I wanted to preserve these important relationships. I wasn't going to just say let's keep in touch, I was going to make a concerted and intentional effort to keep in touch. I immediately put reminders in my calendar from everything to: call your friend' to 'make time to think about who to invite' and even 'write a letter' and 'spend 15 minutes returning text messages'. I wax and wane in my faithfulness to my plan, but when I find I have fallen off track, I get back on or redesign the track to manage a fall.

When we are in the regular mindset of looking after one another, we are spontaneously building connections and empathy through service. This yields long lasting and meaningful relationships with depth. If you want to show someone how to pursue happiness, start your own pursuit! You can't make anyone happy; their feelings come from within. Remember what Shawn Achor taught us: that success comes when you pursue happiness and not the other way around.

Boundaries are essential in healthy relationships. We will discuss this some more in the next book, I'm Non-Traditional. That word *boundaries...* makes me roll my eyes sometimes. The word has lost weight in my life; it's a buzzword that HR-type people use, right? Having good boundaries means you know your social limits, define them, and hold them. My mom has a boundary: no calls after 9 pm. One of my boundaries is that there are no surprise visitors at my home. I chose this boundary because I have learned that it helps me manage my stress, through therapy I learned that the root was some PTSD stuff. I hold that boundary, but I'm able to manage my own emotional wellness relative to the trigger because I'm aware that it exists and I've become willing to consider and accept this about myself, but didn't believe it was true at first. I needed help to work through these ideas, and I still rely on my community to help me understand myself and my limits. Boundaries are essential when we are talking about building healthy relationships at work and preventing unnecessary hurt feelings or disappointments.

I invite you to consider this idea and spend some time on it. Do you have any boundaries now? With whom? How do they know what your boundaries are? How do you know what your boundaries are? Do they change? Are they subjective to certain places and people? Here is some space for notes:

____

____

____

____

____

____

Consistency is key in life, relationships, fitness, nutrition, etc. There is good news and bad news: hard work and consistency are the secret ingredients to good outcomes. Good news because we understand those words and what they mean. Bad news because there isn't a new idea or some new thing you've discovered that you can try that you've never tried before. I sometimes hope, even plan that a new book will be the secret thing that tells me just what I need to know to unlock some vault, some secret answer to life and make everything so much easier. Books, people, TV, news, podcasts… they all help us reflect on ourselves and each other. We need each other to be our best in every capacity. Isn't that so annoying? And also great news, because here we all are together, trying to get along. Be confident in your pursuit of growth and change. Have courage in your service work. Reach for your potential as often as you remember to. Better yet, help everyone around you reach for theirs as often as you can; it's magical.

If you are also passionate about building connections, if you are feeling like SOMETHING needs to change but don't know what? Maybe you have had a good start (or many) on building up the culture at work, but it never takes hold; if you dread going to work or if you feel alone in your struggles: get in touch; I want to help.

All my love,

Emily

References

1. The Happiness Advantage by Shawn Achor
2. Connection by Nicholas Christakis
3. Turn the Ship Around by David Marquet
4. Dare to Lead by Brene Brown
5. Leadership Training 2023 by the Hollaway Group

Made in the USA
Middletown, DE
03 December 2024